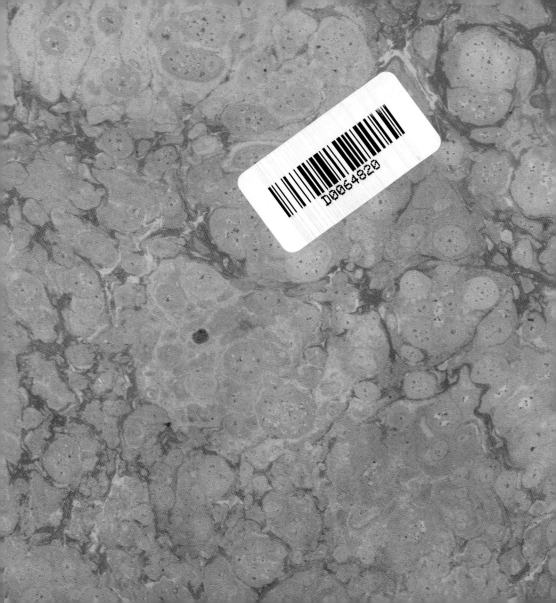

The Gift of a Child

For David, Angus, Joanna, Robert and Icilda — five very special gifts, and for Edward, the first of the next generation

Copyright © 1982 Lion Publishing
This edition copyright © 1994 Lion Publishing

Published by
Lion Publishing plc
Sandy Lane West, Oxford, England
ISBN 0 7459 3004 2
Albatross Books Pty Ltd
PO Box 320, Sutherland, NSW 2232, Australia
ISBN 0 7324 1231 5

First edition 1982

A catalogue record for this book is available from the British Library

Printed and bound in Singapore

Picture acknowledgments
Jon Arnold: Companions; Neil Beer: cover & Love Is, Setting Goals, Forgive Me, Love Means Discipline, Take Time; Image Bank: (Ron Colby) A Prayer for Fathers; Nicholas Rous: Today; Skjold Photography: Energy Gap, Reason to Believe, One of the Family, The Real Me, Letting Go, Tomorrow's Memories; Telegraph Colour Library: (A. Tilley) Sharing Skills; Daniel E. Wray: Nightwatch; ZEFA: (K. Owaki) Your Link with Life, (J. Feingersh) So much to Learn, (P. Barton) Thank You

Text acknowledgments
'Perfect You' and 'So much to Learn' from *Song for Sarah* © 1979 Paula D'Arcy, Harold Shaw Publishers 1979, Lion Publishing 1981; 'Forgive Me' from *I've got to talk to somebody, God* © 1968, 1969 by Marjorie Holmes Mighell, reprinted by permission of Hodder & Stoughton Ltd and Doubleday and Company, Inc; 'Companions' and 'Take Time' ('Don't tell me') from *For the Love of Children* © 1979 Ulrich Schaffer, Lion Publishing 1980; 'Take Time' ('Children take time') from *How do you find the time?* by Pat King, Tyndale House Publishers 1975, by Marjorie Holmes Mighell reprinted by permission of Hodder & Stoughton Ltd and Doubleday and Company, Inc.

The Gift of a
Child

Written and compiled by
Marion Stroud

A LION BOOK

Your Link with Life

Children are a gift from the Lord; they are a real blessing

Jesus... said to his disciples, 'Let the children come to me, and do not stop
them, because the Kingdom of God belongs to such as these...'
Then he took the children in his arms, placed his hands on each of them,
and blessed them.

FROM MARK'S GOSPEL

Mankind owes to the child the best it has to give.

UNITED NATIONS DECLARATION

Before I got married I had six theories about bringing up children;
now I have six children and no theories.

JOHN WILMOT, EARL OF ROCHESTER (1647–80)

A mother clasping her little girl's hand, a father gripping the fingers of his
small son — each is leading his own dreams forward, holding fast to his own
tomorrows... A child's hand in yours... is your link with life itself.

MARJORIE HOLMES

Setting Goals

**Jesus said . . . 'Do not worry about your life,
what you will eat; or about your body, what you
will wear. Life is more than food, and . . .
clothes . . . your Father knows that you need
them. But seek his kingdom . . . and these things
will be given to you as well.'**

Heavenly Father, please give our children the right goals. Keep them from drifting, going with the crowd to gain popularity and friends.

Please enable them to appreciate their strengths and acknowledge their weaknesses. To see their talents and abilities as gifts from yourself, to be treasured, developed and used to serve you, God, and others. Help them to have their priorities right. Then the rest of life will fall into place.

We hardly dare to ask this for them, Father. Life lived this way is the tough option, and because we love them so much we want to protect them from hurt. But you have a good purpose for their lives. You know why you have created them just the way they are, for such a time as this. So we would ask you again Father – please give us and these children of ours, the right goals.

So Much to Learn

Dear Sarah:

What's happening? Why are you crying? And why can't I figure out why you're crying? Who'd have guessed being a parent wasn't easy? . . . What an adjustment from being someone's daughter to also being someone's (your!) mother. It's overwhelming that you depend so totally on me.

In the hospital motherhood all seemed adventurous and exciting. But here at home I'm way too tired to be poetic. Some days it's a contest to see who cries more, you or I. How lucky we are that your daddy is so uncomplaining.

Dear Sarah, do you think we'll make it?

Dear Sarah:

Was I the one who secretly doubted that one little baby could significantly change our lives? . . . I had a lot to learn!

Did I often make it hard for you, those first months? There I was trying to soothe you with one arm, furiously turning the pages of my Dr Spock with the other. It seems so much better now. I'm far from a pro, but I do think I'm getting used to us . . .

PAULA D'ARCY

Night-watch

**People who say they sleep like a baby usually
don't have one!**

Why is it, Lord God, that he seldom wants to sleep when we do? This child
– he's like a human whirlwind in the daytime, and still wakes up at three in
the morning to play. If he were ill or cold or hungry we could soothe him, but
he's just bored, a little lonely, wide-awake.

We've tried the remedies that they've suggested. We've put toys into his cot, a
night-light in his room, fed him, watered him, picked him up, left him to
cry . . . and still we keep night-watch while all around is wrapped in blissful,
peaceful sleep.

We need your help, dear God. Help us to be grateful for his glowing health,
boundless energy and seemingly endless curiosity. Give us the strength we
need to face each new morning; clear thinking for the day's work; patience
with the little problems that loom so large when we are tired, and wisdom so
that we may know just how to meet his needs. And most of all help us to hang
on to the assurance that, as with all of childhood's phases, this too will pass,
and one night we'll all enjoy some quiet, unbroken sleep.

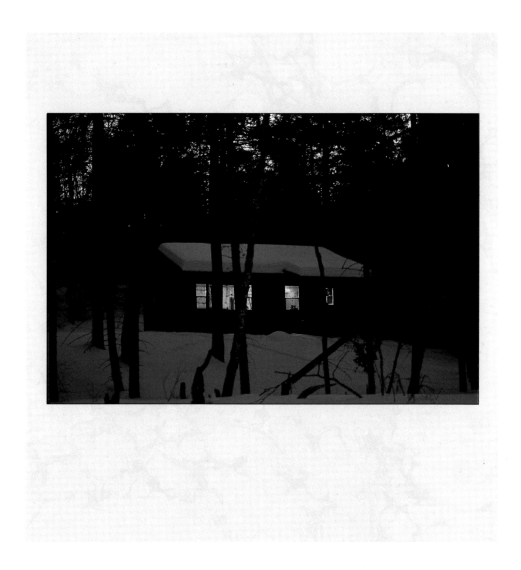

Today

Today you ran circles around the average athlete in training
  scaled more impossible climbs than
    the average mountaineer
talked faster and for longer than the average disc jockey
asked more questions than the average
    quizmaster on a busy day
and untidied the entire house faster than a force 8 gale.

Today you were three years old.

Today I walked one mile and ran at least two
  performed three emergency rescues and four
    minor operations
answered questions on natural history, mechanics,
    astronomy and religion
acted as nursemaid, chauffeur, housekeeper,
    cook and freelance entertainer.

Today I was your mother.

Forgive Me

Oh, God, I was so cross to the children today. Forgive me.

Oh, God, I was so discouraged, so tired. I took it out on them. Forgive me.

Forgive me my bad temper, my impatience, and most of all my yelling. I cringe to think of it. My heart aches. I want to wake them up and beg them to forgive me. Only I can't, it would only upset them more.

I've got to go on living with the memory of this day. My unjust tirades. The guilty fear in their eyes as they flew about trying to appease me. Thinking it all their fault — my troubles, my disappointments.

Dear God, the utter helplessness of children. Their vulnerability before this awful thing, adult power. And how forgiving they are, hugging me at bedtime, kissing me goodnight. And all I can do now is to straighten a cover, move a fallen toy, touch a small head burrowed into a pillow, and beg in my heart, 'Forgive me'.

Lord, in failing these little ones whom you've put into my keeping, I'm failing you. Please let your infinite patience and goodness fill me tomorrow. Stand by me, keep your hand on my shoulder. Don't let me be so cross to my children.

MARJORIE HOLMES

Energy Gap

Dear Lord God, are all six-year-old boys like this — a bundle of noisy, tumbling, talking humanity who is on the move from the moment that he erupts out of bed in the morning until he collapses between the covers at night — unless there are cartoons on television! He has the appetite of a horse, the arguing ability of a barrack-room lawyer, the curiosity of a cat and the lung power of a sergeant-major! He is too big to be babied, but to small to be given much responsibility.

Sometimes, God, he doesn't seem to know how to cope with all that life and energy pent up inside one small body, and since he's as fearless as he's fidgety, he must work his guardian angel overtime! Help him, God. And please help us. Help us to find ways for him to channel his energy; to stretch that developing body and mind in safety. Thank you for school, for gym clubs and swimming pools. Thank you for libraries, for parks and museums and all the things that we can do and discover in our own back garden. Thank you for all the fun he finds in each day. Please help us to enjoy him as he is now — and enable us all to savour the great adventure of being six years old, together.

Love Means Discipline

Teach a child how he should live, and he will remember it all his life.

FROM THE BOOK OF PROVERBS

The child who has everything done for him, everything given to him, and nothing required of him is a deprived child ... The parent who tries to please the child by giving in to him and expecting nothing from him ends up by pleasing no one, least of all the child. For in the end, when trouble results, the child will blame the parent for his gutlessness.

LARRY CHRISTENSON

Discipline is demanded of the athlete to win a game. Discipline is required for the captain running his ship. Discipline is needed for the pianist to practise for the concert. Only in the matter of personal conduct is the need for discipline questioned. But if parents believe standards are necessary, then discipline certainly is needed to attain them.

GLADYS BROOKS

Companions

Lord,
sometimes I am frightened by the
weight I feel
to bring up these children
that you have entrusted to me . . .

I know that I will make mistakes,
that I will fail my children,
that my strength and patience will not be sufficient,
that I will make the wrong decisions,
and that at times my love will grow weak.

Around me I see parents
labouring under the same weight,
afraid in the same way,
trying their best

Help us all to keep love going,
and put your blessing on our love
which then has a chance to overcome
all the mistakes we will make.

ULRICH SCHAFFER

Reason to Believe

Many parents do nothing about their children's religious education, telling them they can decide what they believe when they're twenty-one. That's like telling them they can decide when they're twenty-one whether or not they should brush their teeth. By then, their teeth may have fallen out. Likewise, their principles and morality may also be non-existent.

PRINCESS GRACE OF MONACO

Remember this! . . . Love the Lord your God with all your heart, with all your soul, and with all your strength. Never forget these commands. Teach them to your children . . . In time to come your children will ask you, 'Why did the Lord our God command us to obey all these laws?' Then tell them . . .

FROM THE BOOK OF DEUTERONOMY

Don't forget what I teach you, my son. . . . Trust in the Lord with all your heart. Remember the Lord in everything you do, and he will show you the right way. Never let yourself think that you are wiser than you are; simply obey the Lord and refuse to do wrong . . . When the Lord corrects you, my son, pay close attention and take it as a warning. The Lord corrects those he loves, as a father corrects a son of whom he is proud.

FROM THE BOOK OF PROVERBS

Take Time

**Don't tell me how much you love me;
show me by having time for me.**

Children take time. Therein lies the problem . . . children take so much time.

It's easy to see why we may have a problem. All these things that must be done with our children are at war with all that society tells us or that we tell ourselves we must do elsewhere . . .

For me the war ended abruptly with the realization that I didn't have to be a great housekeeper or an enviable cook . . . I didn't have to be the politically involved, the champion of the downtrodden or even the exciting, innovative hostess.

If we have been called by God to be mothers, let's drop all the activities that are making it so painful for us to enjoy our children. For everyone who says, 'But society needs me.' I would say, 'Let's give our children the time they need to help them grow into secure people'. We are adding a greater burden to society than we could ever compensate for with all our good deeds if we don't.

PAT KING

One of the Family

Not flesh of my flesh,
Not bone of my bone,
But still miraculously my own.
Never forget for a single minute
You didn't grow under my heart, but in it.

To me you are special.
The fact that I didn't give birth to you
doesn't make me less of a mother,
or you my daughter.
For mothering is more than birth,
and growing is something
that we can experience together . . .
I longed for you,
And when at last you were chosen,
we were a family.
I see mirrored in your personality
a reflection of our own ways.
And a bond has been created —
of love, warmth and security.

CLAIRE SHORT

The Real Me

My mother wishes that I could be more organized and less messy – so that she would be thought to be a good housekeeper and our house an 'ideal home'.

My father wishes that I would get good marks at school, so that he could talk about me to his friends at work, and be thought a successful father.

My grandparents wish that I was younger so that I could be babied, or older, with more achievements, so that they could be proud grandparents.

My teacher wishes that I would be quiet and not ask awkward questions, so that she could be a good teacher without much effort.

My coach wishes that I would be a good player so that his team would win.

I wish that they would encourage me to do well what I can do. I wish that they would stop blaming me for failing to do what I have no ability to do, and allow me to branch out, experiment and explore.

I wish that they could be there when I need them, and yet set me free to discover for myself who I am, why I am here and where I am going.

I wish that I was sure that they loved me, the real me, just as I am, here and now.

Sharing Skills

It would be so much easier to do it myself. To avoid the grumbles, the arguments and the reminders. The calling you back to do it again . . . and again . . . and again, until it is right.

It would be so much quicker to do it my way; to avoid having to stop to show you how things work, where the tools are, what the recipe means. There would be fewer mistakes, less mess, fewer breakages and fewer squabbles about whose turn it is. But there would also be no new skills acquired for the future, no satisfaction in a job well done, and no sense of sharing, caring and being involved. For responsibility is a skill which, like any other, has to be learned.

A Prayer for Fathers

God bless fathers, all fathers old and young.

Bless the new father holding his son or daughter in his arms for the first time. Give him the strength to provide for its physical needs. But even more, give him the love to provide for its hungering heart.

Give him time and the will to be its friend. Give him wisdom, patience, justice in discipline. Make him a hero in his youngster's eyes. So that the word Father will always mean a fair and mighty man.

And God bless older fathers too. Fathers who are weary from working for their young. Fathers whose children don't turn out the way they'd hoped; children who seem thoughtless, ungrateful, critical, children who rebel.

Bless those fathers, Lord; comfort them.

And stay close to all these fathers when they must tell sons and daughters goodbye. When kids leave home, fathers need to be steadied too, Lord. (Mothers aren't the only ones who cry.)

You, our Heavenly Father, must surely understand these earthly fathers well. In your infinite love (and infinite experience!) bless fathers, all fathers old and young.

MARJORIE HOLMES

Letting Go

**Give your children up to God . . . it is utterly safe
to place your children in God's sure hands.**

'I'll be back', he said, 'sometime!'

*And with that he left; a rebel, rejecting education, a job — with or without
prospects — belonging; just another gesture of nonconformity from a boy who
has always seemed compelled to be desperately and defiantly different.*

*His mother would have argued, pleaded with him, tried to persuade him to
give things one more try.*

*But I let him go: Lord God, I had to let him go. For that is what you, the
Father of all, do with us. You could have made us puppets, but instead you
gave us freedom. And I knew that the time has come to give that to him — the
dignity of choice, and the responsibility to live with the consequences of that
choice. Be with him in that 'far country', wherever it is. If, like that prodigal
in the Bible, he ends up starving and destitute, remind him that our door
stands open for his return. And when that day comes, Father, help me to
welcome him back with the same open-hearted accepting love that you offer —
to us both.*

Thank You

Thank you, God, for this family — just for once all seated at the breakfast-table at the same time, brushed and bright-eyed, ready and eager for a new day.

Thank you that on this sparkling sunny morning no one has fought for possession of the newspaper, spilled the coffee, burnt the toast or tripped over the dog.

Thank you that the beginning of this day is not marred by fear of a test, a feud with a friend or homework mislaid.

Thank you for cheerful conversation, help given, unasked, and a kiss in passing from a son who long since thought himself too big for such displays of affection.

Thank you, God for this family. Thank you that as well as the expense, the worries and the grey Mondays, we have days like this: jewel-bright, filled with love and laughter. Help me to appreciate it now and remember it later when the storms blow up again. And today and every day — thank you, God, for this family.

Tomorrow's Memories

**Today you are creating tomorrow's memories.
Invest in positive memories, for childhood
memories mould the person of the future.**

*Last month, Dad was kept late at the office and forgot to phone and let Mum know.
Last month, Mum was mad with him, and snapped and snarled at the rest of us.
Last month, someone broke the window, and no one would own up.
Last month, Gran was ill, we overslept three mornings in a row, and lost one pair of
shoes and two lots of homework.
I think that last month is best forgotten, but Dad says 'No'. He says that last month
we learned what not to do, and that is a memory well worth keeping.*

*Last week, a rare snowfall transformed our world into a winter wonderland.
And we just left the dirty dishes in the sink, the house not tidied, weekend
chores undone. Not for the sake of business calls or family crises, but so that
we could build a family of fat snow people, lining the garden path like ghostly
guards as darkness fell. And now the snow is gone, but not the chores. Jostling
with others, they demand attention still. So were those carefree hours time
lost? No, rather they were time invested — in a memory.*

Love Is...

Love is . . . *pacing the floor through the hours after midnight, soothing your crying with love-words and lullabies, when all of my being is begging for rest.*

Love is . . . a painting of a scarlet giant with no arms and a single eye, bearing that heart-stopping legend in wobbly letters: 'My Mummy is best'.

Love is . . . reading the same story over and over and not missing any of it out.

Love is . . . the last sticky sweet in the bag, only faintly dusted with dirt and dog-hairs, resolutely not eaten, because you had decided to keep it for me.

Love is . . . learning new skills so that we can help you to develop yours.

Love is . . . tepid tea and a soggy biscuit placed tenderly by our bed at 6.30 a.m., so that I don't have to get up early on my birthday.

Love is . . . caring enough to say 'no', even if 'everybody else is doing it'.

Love is . . . letting you go with a lump in my throat, a prayer in my heart and a smile on my face, as you stride out of the door to take on the world.

Love is . . . struggling to share the faith that is our sure foundation, so that you, a child of the present, can have light for the future.